eGrade

Student Learning Guide for Calculus

BRADBURY FRANKLIN
University of Nebraska - Lincoln

JOHN L. ORR
University of Nebraska - Lincoln

JOHN WILEY & SONS, INC.
New York / Chichester / Weinheim / Brisbane / Singapore / Toronto

PUBLISHER	Peter Janzow
ASSISTANT EDITOR	Penny Perrotto
MARKETING MANAGER	Catherine Beckham
SUPPLEMENTS MANAGER	Marsheela Evans
SENIOR DESIGNER	Harry Nolan

To order books or for customer service call 1-800-CALL-WILEY (225-5945)

ISBN 0-471-39591-9

Printed in the United States of America

10 9 8 7 6 5 4 3 2 1

Printed and bound by Von Hoffman Graphics, Inc.

PREFACE

This **Student Learning Guide for Calculus** is intended to help you get started using the *eGrade* On-Line Assessment System. It will show you how to take full advantage of *eGrade*'s unique features as you work on quizzes, homework, exams and tutorials over the World Wide Web. *eGrade* was developed to help students in the following ways:

- *eGrade* enables you to work on many different versions of your assignment, to receive immediate feedback on your work, and to control your final grade. If you don't like the grade you get the first time, keep trying until you reach the level of success you desire!

- *You* choose the time and place that suits you best to work on your calculus tutorials, homework, quizzes and exams. With *eGrade* you have more freedom in your studies and you can reduce your exam anxiety.

- *eGrade* emphasizes mastery and accuracy in learning. At the same time, *eGrade* offers you the flexibility and practice you need to attain these goals and to get a sense of meaningful accomplishment at the end of the course.

- Working at a computer is becoming a larger part of people's working lives. Use *eGrade* to learn to interact successfully with computers and with the Internet and enhance your working skills for the future!

We sincerely hope that your work with *eGrade* will be fun and successful and that your accomplishments on *eGrade* in your class will be a useful rung in the ladder of academic success.

To access the anonymous practice calculus tutorials, please visit the John Wiley & Sons website at www.wiley.com/college/egrade/calculus.

CONTENTS

CHAPTER **1**

Getting Started With eGrade

CHAPTER OUTLINE

1.1   WELCOME!

Welcome to *eGrade*! You are about to join the thousands of students for whom this web-based assignment system has proven to be a powerful learning tool! You can use *eGrade* to do homework or quizzes, to learn in tutorial sessions, or even to take exams in your course. Because *eGrade* handles many different types of assessment, we use the catchall phrase "assignment" for all the different types of work you might do on *eGrade*.

1.2   HOW TO USE THIS GUIDE

The goal of this guide is to make using *eGrade* as easy, fun, and effective for you as possible. You will find that time spent reading this guide pays big dividends in using *eGrade*. However, if you are the type of person who likes to jump right in and get your feet wet, read these sections right now: 1.3, 1.4, 1.5, 2.2, and 3.1. Also make sure to read the boxes containing helpful hints that are found in each chapter.

1.3   SYSTEM REQUIREMENTS FOR *eGRADE*

Whether you are using *eGrade* within your school or you access the John Wiley & Sons calculus tutorials directly, to use *eGrade* you need access to the World Wide Web and a web browser. Netscape Navigator® version 4.0 or later, or Microsoft Internet Explorer® version 5.0 or later are the best browsers for using *eGrade*. However, earlier versions of these browsers will work for most of *eGrade's* features, as will other browsers. Your browser options for Java and JavaScript should be "on".

1.4   THE *eGRADE* STUDENT HOME PAGE AT YOUR SCHOOL

Your instructor will either place a link to the *eGrade* Student Home Page on the course page for your class or give you a web address for the *eGrade* Student Home Page at your school. You'll know you have arrived there when you see a web page like Figure 1.1. It's a good idea to bookmark the *eGrade* Student Home Page. To do this, use the "Favorites" button on Internet Explorer, or the "Bookmarks" button on Netscape.

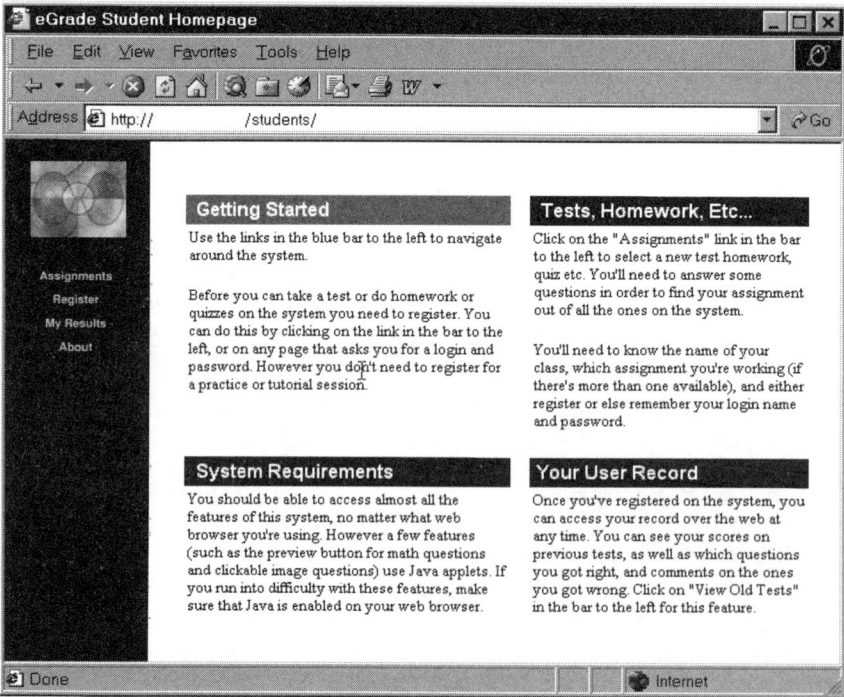

Figure 1.1 The *eGrade* Student Home Page.

Use the links on the blue bar at the side of the *eGrade* Student Home Page to reach each of the main functions of *eGrade*: registering (**Register**), working assignments (**Assignments**), and viewing your results (**My Results**).

1.5   REGISTERING FOR YOUR CLASS WITH *eGRADE*

Before you can take assignments on *eGrade*, you must register for your class on *eGrade*. To do this, go to the *eGrade* Student Home Page and follow the link for **Register**.

When you register with *eGrade* you will enter your name, your student ID and your email address (if you have one). At the same time you choose the login name and password that you'll use to access your *eGrade* assignments in this class.

Registration Form

In order to take a test for credit, or to record a score, you need to register with the system. To do this, please fill out the information requested in the form below.

Choose a login name: jdoe — *Choose a short, easy to remember login name; for example, your first initial and your last name*

Choose a password: ******** — *Keep this password secret to protect your confidential record.*

Retype your password: ******** — *Retype your password to make sure you typed it right the first time.*

Your name: John R Doe (First Name / MI / Last Name)

Your student ID Number: 123456789

Your email address: jdoe11@stdnts.univeeu.edu — *Optionally, you can enter your email address here.*

Your class:
Astronomy 103 - Lee
Bios 202
Chemistry 109 - Carr
Chemistry 109 - George
Chemistry 110 at 8:30 - McLaughlin
Chemistry 110 at 9:30 - McLaughlin
Math 102 - 1:30 Koetz
Select the name of the class you're in from the drop-down list.

Press to enter your information: Press to continue

Figure 1.2 The *eGrade* Registration Page

Here are the steps you need to take to register for your class on your school's *eGrade*:

1. Choose a **login name** and enter it in the box on the registration form. Most people like to choose either a nickname for themselves or their first initial followed by their last name. Your login name must be between 3 and 8 letters ('a' to 'z') or numbers ('0' to '9'). Your login must begin with a letter, and spaces are not allowed.

2. Choose a **password** and type it into the password box on the form. For security reasons it won't appear, and you must carefully retype it in the second password box.

    > *Make sure you remember your login name and password. You'll need to use them every time you log on to work on an assignment in this class. But if you do forget them, see Appendix A to learn how eGrade can remind you.*

3. Enter your **full name**, and, if your school has assigned you a **student ID number** (it may be your social security number), you enter it now.

4. If you have an **e-mail address**, enter it into the box on the form. Please double-check to make sure it is valid! This email address serves a dual purpose:
    (i) it enables the instructor to respond to questions about your work on *eGrade*, and;
    (ii) it enables *eGrade* to send you the password should you forget it.

5. Press the button labeled "Press to continue" at the *bottom* of the page to enter your information.

You will then be given a chance to review the data you entered. If it is correct, click "OK" at the top of the page. Click "Back" to make any corrections.

As soon as you have successfully registered for your class, you'll be given a chance to take your first assignment. The next chapter discusses how to work assignments with *eGrade*.

> *If you are in a large class or in a class with multiple sections, make absolutely certain that you are registering for the right section.*

1.6   USING eGRADE CALCULUS TUTORIALS AT JOHN WILEY

As a supplement to your textbook, the publisher is providing free, *eGrade* calculus tutorials on the web. Visit the John Wiley & Sons website at www.wiley.com/college/egrade/calculus to access tutorials within all of the major calculus topics. No grades will be recorded or tracked, but you will be asked to create your own login and password before accessing the tutorials.

> *The calculus tutorials are independent of any assignments that your instructor may be offering within your school server.*

As with all of *eGrade*, the calculus tutorials will give you immediate feedback on your work. Therefore, these tutorials are an excellent way to review material from precalculus, see example problems, drill topics which have given you trouble, and practice for an exam. In addition, if your instructor uses the complete *eGrade* software for your homework, quizzes, or tests, the anonymous tutorials can help you get comfortable with the system navigation and syntax (see Appendix B for more details on math syntax).

CHAPTER **2**

Starting An *eGrade* Assignment

CHAPTER OUTLINE

2.1 When Best To Take An Assignment
2.2 Starting An Assignment

2.3 Restrictions On Taking Assignments
2.4 Choosing The Assignment Type

2.1 WHEN BEST TO TAKE AN ASSIGNMENT

Since working on an *eGrade* assignment involves using the World Wide Web (WWW), you may find that *eGrade* moves slowly sometimes. This may be because of heavy traffic, or because the system itself is being asked to do a lot of things at once. The WWW and campus computer labs tend to be busier in the evenings, so you may want to work on your assignments at other times of day. Since it is well known that technical problems and heavy traffic are common with the internet, instructors often have little sympathy for the students who run into difficulty because they left their assignment to the last minute.

> *To avoid heavy traffic, complete your eGrade assignments well before the deadline! If you do find it slow going, please do not click repeatedly while waiting — this slows eGrade even more!*

2.2   STARTING AN ASSIGNMENT

To start an assignment, go to the Student Home Page and click on the **Assignments** button on the vertical blue bar at the left (see Figure 1.1). To choose your assignment, you need to:

1. **Select your class** from the menu listing all classes on the system.

2. **Choose the assignment** you want to take from the menu of assignments in your class.

You can only work on one assignment at a time. If there is an assignment you were working on but never had graded, you'll be given three options before you start a new assignment:

- **Abandon the old assignment**. If you choose this option, the work you did on the old assignment will be lost, so be sure this is really what you want to do!

- **Grade the assignment**. This will enter a grade report for the assignment exactly as if you had it graded while you were last working on it.

- **Resume working on the old assignment**. You may need special permission to do this after a long delay.

2.3   RESTRICTIONS ON TAKING ASSIGNMENTS

Your instructor can impose access restrictions on assignments. One common restriction is a limit on the number of tries that you are allowed. Other restrictions include limiting the number of tries per day or requiring that you have passed certain other assignments before you can work on the one you are interested in.

If you don't meet the restrictions for the assignment you have selected, you will be blocked from entering and told about the restrictions. For example, if there is a restriction on taking Quiz 3 more than five times, and you are trying to take it for the sixth time, you will be blocked by a screen that reminds you of the policy.

2.4   CHOOSING THE ASSIGNMENT TYPE

Your instructor can set *eGrade* assignments in one of five assignment types. Depending on which type of assignment you've been given, you may have time limits, access restrictions, etc. If your instructor has enabled more than one type for a given assignment, you will be asked to choose between the available types: "Practice," "Homework," "Proctored Exam," "Study Session," or "Mastery." Table 2.1 gives a breakdown of these assignment types:

Table 2.1 Summary of Assignment Types

Assignment Type / Features	Practice	Homework/ Quiz	Proctored Exam	Study Session	Mastery
Login required		X	X		X
Permanent record kept		X	X		X
May have access restrictions		X	X		X
May have a time limit		X	X		X
May be pass/no pass	X	X	X		
Questions graded one at a time				X	X
Take from anywhere	X	X		X	X

> *If you want to receive credit for an assignment, make certain that you do not select a "Practice" assignment. Work done on "Practice" assignments is not recorded by eGrade!*

CHAPTER **3**

Completing An *eGrade* Assignment

CHAPTER OUTLINE

3.1   ACADEMIC RULES AND *eGRADE*

All of the academic rules of your school are in full force when you are using eGrade!

> *Using eGrade does not alter your school's academic rules or honor codes. Breaking these rules can result in serious penalties.*

3.2   NAVIGATING THROUGH AN ASSIGNMENT

Use the *eGrade* navigation buttons at the top of each page to move backward and forward between the pages of your assignment.

> *Never use your browser's buttons to navigate in eGrade! You may cause a system error. If this occurs please see Appendix A.*

Table 3.1 *eGrade* Navigation Buttons

	Page backward or forward.
	Jump to a certain page of the assignment.
	Save your work and continue working on the assignment.
	Undo the last change on the current page.
	Submit the assignment for grading.
	Exit for now, but save your work to finish later.

In the upper left corner of every page you will also see three useful buttons:

Table 3.2 *eGrade* Quick Start and Help Buttons

	Jump to the Student Home Page.
	Start a new assignment.
	Get help!

3.3 A MATTER OF TIME

Some assignments are timed. If your assignment is being timed, you will see a message such as "Remaining time: 54 minutes" on each page of your assignment.

> *Be mindful of the time limit (if any) on your assignment and remember that the clock keeps ticking when you are logged off!*

If you leave your assignment idle for too long, you will get an error message telling you that you have been logged out for security reasons. If this happens, your work will be saved by *eGrade* and you can log back in and continue working on your assignment (unless the assignment was timed and the time is up). None of your work will be lost!

> *If you leave your assignment idle for too long, you will get a message that you have been logged out and must re—login.*

3.4 THE *eGRADE* QUESTION STYLES

There are a variety of *eGrade* question styles. An overview of these styles and how to answer them is given in Table 3.3. If your instructor gives you guidelines on how to answer *eGrade* questions, you should carefully follow those as well.

Table 3.3 Overview of Question/Answer Styles

Question Style	Directions & Example
Multiple Choice	Click on one or more buttons to select the correct items from the list.
	Which of the following are reptiles? () Snake () Cat () Cow () Iguana
Menu	Click on menus to select phrases to fill the blanks in the text or to select matching items in a pair of lists.
	The capital of California is ⟨Sacramento / San Diego / Los Angeles (Choose one)⟩ and ⟨Sacramento / San Diego / Los Angeles (Choose one)⟩ is the largest city in California.
Short Answer	Enter a word or phrase.
	Who was the president during the Civil War? _____
Clickable Image	Click on the correct "hotspot" in an image displayed on the page.
	Click on the state of Nebraska in the map of the US below…
Essay	Enter your essay into the text box. Since spelling and grammar may be counted, you may want to compose your essay in your word processor with spelling/grammar checking and then copy and paste in your answer. Your work will be graded later by your instructor.
	Describe a significant event in your life.
Formula / Numeric	Requires an answer involving numbers and/or variables, possibly an equation or a list. Read instructions carefully. See Sections 3.4 & 3.5 and Appendix B for more details.
	What is the derivative of sin(3x)?

3.5   ANSWERING FORMULA QUESTIONS

Some questions require an answer involving numbers and/or variables. There are several types of these — you may be asked for a formula, a number without units, a number with units, a list of formulas, or an equation. We refer to all of these as "formula questions". When answering a formula question, read the question carefully and look for instructions under the answer box for information about what format is expected in your answer.

> *eGrade expects you to enter your answer very accurately.*
> *Omissions or slips that may seem minor can be costly!*

3.5.1   MATHEMATICAL EXPRESSIONS

eGrade recognizes mathematical expressions written in standard calculator format; any mathematical formula that the Texas Instruments TI-85 will graph, *eGrade* understands. Here are a few examples:

$$\texttt{x\^{}2-2x+1} \qquad \texttt{2sin(x)} \qquad \texttt{(x\^{}2+1)e\^{}(-x\^{}2)}$$

A common error is misplaced or missing parentheses. It is important to respect the order of operations. Division takes precedence over addition, so if you want to express addition before division, use parentheses for grouping. For example, if you want to enter

$$\frac{x+3}{2}$$

you must type $\texttt{(x+3)/2}$, not $\texttt{x+3/2}$. Likewise, $\texttt{3e\^{}2x}$ represents

$$3e^2 x$$

while $\texttt{3e\^{}(2x)}$ represents

$$3e^{2x}$$

To help you avoid this kind of error, *eGrade* can show you what it understands from the answer you typed. There is a button marked **Preview** beside every formula-entry box, which will bring up a popup window showing your answer expressed in standard mathematical layout. The first time that you use the preview button during each session it may take a while to come up since it needs to load a large Java program — subsequent uses are much faster.

> Use the **Preview** button beside formula—entry boxes to
> make sure you've used the right syntax to express your ideas.

Two other common slips to avoid are:

- Using e (which stands for Euler's constant, 2.718...) instead of E in scientific notation. To express 6×10^{23}, you should use `6E23` or `6*10^23`— do not use `6e23`.

- Use of commas in numerical answers. Commas are not allowed in numbers — write `1232` not `1,232`.

If you struggle with entering formula answers correctly, keep in mind that your ability to express the answers in standard math syntax is an important measure of your understanding of the formulas.

eGrade accepts any answer that is mathematically equivalent to the correct answer. [1] Thus if the correct answer is $(x+2)^2$ and you write `x^2+2x+1`, your answer is still graded as correct. Because *eGrade* requires exact numerical precision (unless your instructor has allowed inexact answers — see Section B.2), you should leave mathematical expressions unevaluated and refer to the constants `e` and `pi` by name. For instance, if the correct answer is `pi/3` and you write `3.14159/3` or `1.047` you will not receive credit. Refer to Appendix B for more details on entering formulas.

3.5.2   UNITS

eGrade can recognize a wide variety of units and equivalents. It knows that `1 kg` is `1000 g`, and even knows more complicated facts, such as that `1 N` is `1 kg*m/s^2`. Thus the answer `2.3 kg` will be graded as correct when the correct answer is `2300 g`. Note that *eGrade* will not accept units with a period at the end of them — so in the above example the answer `2300 g.` would be graded as incorrect.

The surest road to receiving credit for your answer is to *strictly follow* your instructor's policy about which units are acceptable and *carefully read* any instructions within the question that describe how to construct your answer.

Note that units that tell what is being measured are *not* used by *eGrade*. Do not write `2.3 g of water`; write `2.3 g` instead.

---

[1] There is one exception to this rule: in the special case of "Restricted" formula mode, trigonometric functions are not accepted. For example instead of "`sin(pi/3)`" you must write "`sqrt(2)/3`".

3.6 GRADING YOUR ASSIGNMENT

When you've completed your assignment, click on the "Grade" button at the top right side of the page. *eGrade* will proofread your assignment to make sure that you have answered all of the questions and will check for certain typos such as missing parentheses in formula answers. If *eGrade* finds any such problems, it will warn you and give you a report on the questions that need your attention. You can then return to your assignment to fix the problems.

If you want to make a change, either click on the "Back" button or select a question on the report that *eGrade* presents to you. If you are certain that you do not want to make any changes, then select "Grade the test anyway".

> *Note that any answers that eGrade warns you about and you do not change will* certainly *be graded as* incorrect.

Once you have successfully submitted an assignment to *eGrade* for grading, it is immediately graded (except for any essay questions, which your instructor will grade later). *eGrade* will tell you your grade and whether you passed or failed (if the assignment was pass/no pass — see Section 2.4). You will then be asked if you want to see your graded assignment. If you do, *eGrade* will show you the correct answers along with your wrong answers, if any. You will also see any explanations that the instructor has provided for wrong answers.

If you have questions about the problems or solutions, it is a good idea to print out the graded assignment and bring it to your instructor, or email your instructor with the assignment name and question number and the approximate time of your assignment. Both you and your instructor can view all of your work on *eGrade*, and your instructor can even make comments on your work that you can view later on, as we describe in Section4.1.

CHAPTER 4

Getting Results From *eGrade*

CHAPTER OUTLINE

4.1 Your Student Record
4.2 Studying Smart With *eGrade* at Your School
4.3 *eGrade* Challenges And Rewards

4.1 YOUR STUDENT RECORD

You can review all of your work in *eGrade* (along with any instructor comments on it) by clicking on the **My Results** button on the Student Home Page. This brings you to your *eGrade* Student Record (see Figure 4.1 below). From here you can view one of your old assignments by selecting it and clicking on **See Details** on the blue bar at the top of the page. Note that you can also click on the blue bar to change your **Password** and review any **Messages** that your instructor has sent you in *eGrade*.

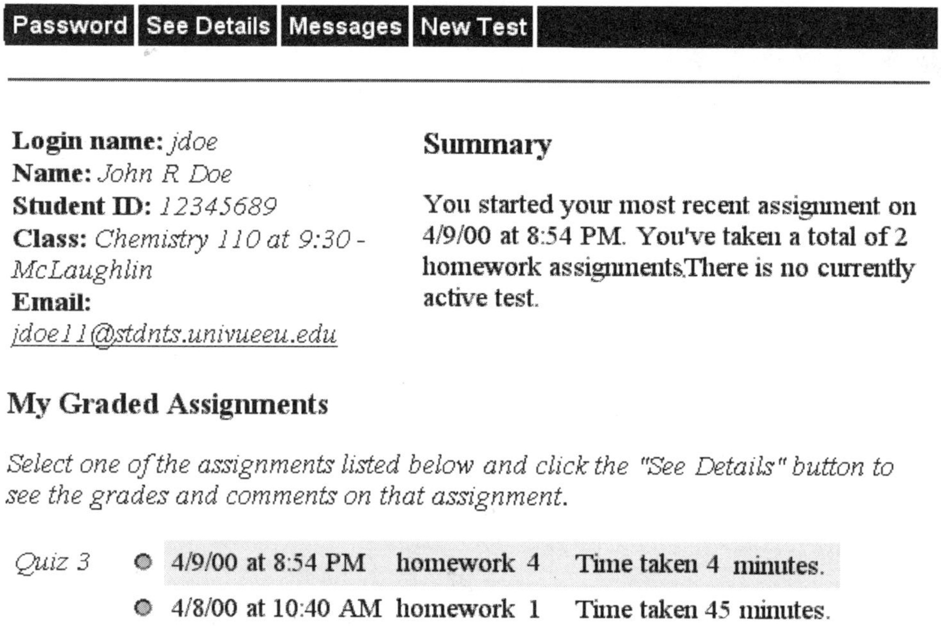

18

```
Password | See Details | Messages | New Test
```

Login name: *jdoe*
Name: *John R Doe*
Student ID: *12345689*
Class: *Chemistry 110 at 9:30 -
McLaughlin*
Email:
jdoe11@stdnts.univueeu.edu

Summary

You started your most recent assignment on 4/9/00 at 8:54 PM. You've taken a total of 2 homework assignments.There is no currently active test.

My Graded Assignments

Select one of the assignments listed below and click the "See Details" button to see the grades and comments on that assignment.

Quiz 3 ◎ 4/9/00 at 8:54 PM   homework 4   Time taken 4 minutes.

◎ 4/8/00 at 10:40 AM homework 1   Time taken 45 minutes.

Figure 4.1 Your *eGrade* Student Record

4.2   STUDYING SMART WITH *eGRADE* AT YOUR SCHOOL

eGrade has been shown to be an effective learning tool for students. Like any learning tool, however, *eGrade* can be used well or poorly. When your instructor decided to use *eGrade*, he or she gave you a greater degree of freedom in your study habits. With freedom comes the responsibility to choose wisely.

Suppose that two students, Gwen and Amy, have been asked to complete an *eGrade* homework assignment for their class. The instructor has given them five tries to make the best score possible out of 10 points.

Amy decides that to get through the quiz in a hurry, she will try the quiz two or three times and hope that she gets some easy questions. Then, if that fails, she will do the best she can on the last couple of quizzes.

First Gwen does the reading to familiarize herself with the material covered by the quiz, then she tries the quiz. She uses the feedback from the problems she got wrong on her first attempt to review the material in the text and in her notes that she needs to understand better. Gwen then tries the quiz a couple more times. If Gwen still does not get the grade she desires, or if she wants more practice, she studies some more or goes to see her instructor before trying the quiz one or two more times.

Clearly Gwen is more likely to learn from the assignment than Amy is, and as a result to perform better on this assignment and on other assignments in the class.

Since there are different study habits and learning styles, you may not follow Gwen's example. When deciding how to study with *eGrade*, however, keep in mind that many students have found that *eGrade* helps them to diagnose and remedy their weaknesses with the material in the class.

Another important thing to keep in mind when using eGrade is the purpose that your instructor has for the *eGrade* assignments. If your instructor hasn't made this purpose clear to you, it would be a good idea to ask!

Questions to ask your instructor about how *eGrade* is used in your class:

- "How do the *eGrade* assignments relate to the other quizzes and exams in terms of types of problems, difficulty level, and material covered?"

- "Am I allowed to work with other students on the *eGrade* assignments?"

- "Am I allowed to use class materials while working on *eGrade* assignments?"

4.3   *eGRADE* CHALLENGES AND REWARDS

At first there may be things about *eGrade* that you find difficult or frustrating. Some students have difficulty with the way *eGrade* requires every part of the answer to be correct in order to receive credit, especially if there are different expectations in other parts of the course. Others are unfamiliar with computers or do not like using them to work assignments. While these represent significant challenges to certain students, it is often these same students who find *eGrade* most rewarding as they meet these challenges.

As you adjust to this new learning tool, remember that finding accurate answers and successfully interacting with computers are important skills in science and business. We hope you will find that using *eGrade* brings you success in your class and in your career!

APPENDIX **A**

Help!

Q: *I've forgotten my password!*

If you are told your password is wrong after several attempts to login, check to make sure that you didn't accidentally turn "Caps Lock" on.

If you have forgotten your login and/or password, please select your class and assignment as if you were going to work on an assignment. When you reach the login screen, follow the link for forgotten passwords to have the system email the necessary information to you.

If you do not receive an email soon after you do this, ask your instructor to give you a new *eGrade* password. Please do *not* create a new student record by registering again. If you do this, your instructor will have to search through multiple records to find all of your grades, and you may not receive credit for some of your assignments!

Q: *Why won't eGrade let me start an assignment?*

If you are being told that you have not satisfied a restriction for the assignment, see Section 2.3. If you are being told that you have an old assignment, see Section 2.2.

Q: *Will I lose my work if my computer hangs up or my browser crashes?*

If either of these things happen, the most that you will lose is your work on the most recent page, since *eGrade* saves each page of your work as you go along. Just login again and choose to continue your last assignment (see Section 2.2).

Q: *What should I do if I get a system error?*

Do not panic. *eGrade* saves your work when you move between pages, so you will not lose more than the last page you were working on.

If you had clicked on your browser's "Back" button before you got the error message, try clicking on your browser's "Forward" button (likewise, if you had clicked on "Forward", try using your browser's "Back" button now), to get back to an earlier page of your assignment. If this fails, then log back in to the assignment and choose to "Resume the old assignment" as described in Section 2.2. To prevent this problem in the future, never use your browser's buttons in *eGrade*! (See Section 3.2 for details on navigating in *eGrade*.)

Q: *Can I view my old assignments? Can my instructor view them?*

Yes, both you and your instructor can view your old work. See Section 4.1.

Q: *What are those question marks doing in the correct answers?*

Those question marks are telling *eGrade* to accept inexact answers. See Appendix B.

Q: *What should I do if I think I've been incorrectly/unfairly graded?*

First, read very carefully through Sections 3.4 & 3.5 and work the formula grading exercise in Appendix B. If you still believe that your answer was not graded correctly, please contact your instructor. Your instructor can view your assignment on *eGrade*.

Q: *What should I do if eGrade is really slow?*

Most important is what *not* to do. Do not click repeatedly on a button. Clicking multiple times just slows the server down even more. Please be patient. In the future, try to use the system at low—use times, and don't wait until the last minute to do your assignments.

Q: *What should I do if the Preview button is not working correctly?*

The Preview button may take a long time to load the first time. Please be patient. If you think that the Preview button is not working, make sure that you have enabled Java and JavaScript on your web browser.

Q: *What should I do if one of the questions is not loading correctly?* If you find that only certain questions are not loading correctly, make sure that you have enabled Java and JavaScript on your web browser.

APPENDIX **B**

Giving Formula Answers

B.1 MATHEMATICAL FUNCTIONS AND OPERATIONS

In Table B.1 is a summary of the mathematical functions and operations in *eGrade*.

Table B.1 Mathematical Functions and Operations

Numbers & Scientific Notation		Arithmetic Operations	
e	e = 2.71828...	+	Addition
pi	pi = 3.14159...	-	Subtraction
2.9E8	e.g. 290,000,000	*	Multiplication
		/	Division
		^	Exponentiation

Trigonometric Functions		Miscellaneous Functions	
sin	Sine	sqrt	Square Root
cos	Cosine	log	Logarithm Base 10
tan	Tangent	ln	Natural Logarithm
arcsin	Inverse Sine	abs	Absolute Value
arccos	Inverse Cosine		
arctan	Inverse Tangent		
sec	Secant		
csc	Cosecant		
cot	Cotangent		

B.2 INEXACT ANSWERS

eGrade requires exact numerical precision unless told otherwise by the instructor (see Section 3.5.1). If the instructor wants to allow for some inexactness in your answer, he or she may give *eGrade* instructions at the end of the correct answer. For example, if the correct answer is "42.3 kg (1 ? .02)", the "(1 ? .02)" allows for any answer within 2% of the correct answer to be accepted, so *eGrade* accepts any answer between 41.554 kg and 43.146 kg. Similarly, if the correct answer is "42.3 kg ? .4 kg", any answer between 41.9 kg and 42.7 kg will be graded as correct. You should never put a "?" in your answer!

B.3 EXERCISE ON FORMULA GRADING

In Table B.2, which of the student answers is incorrect and why? Answers are located at the bottom of the page. [2]

Table B.2 Exercise on Formula Grading

Student's Answer	Correct Answer	Is the Student's Answer Correct? If Not, Why Not?
62.O kJ	62.0 kJ (1 ? .02)	*No. The student used the letter "O", instead of the number "0".*
87.54 ml of water	87.54 ml	**1)**
1.53 g	1.46 g (1 ? .02)	**2)**
0.0710 s.	0.0710 s (1 ? .02)	**3)**
4.31e2	431	**4)**
1,321 kg	1321 kg	**5)**
1.422E 5 J	1.43E5 J (1 ? .03)	**6)**
1.422E2 kJ	1.43E5 J (1 ? .03)	**7)**
1.414	sqrt(2)	**8)**
1.41E5 J	sqrt(2)*10^5 J (1 ? .02)	**9)**

---

[2] Answers to Formula Grading Exercise: **1)** *No, the "of water" is not accepted.* **2)** *No, 1.53 is not within 2% of 1.46.* **3)** *No, the period after the "s" is incorrect.* **4)** *No, e stands for 2.7182... (use E instead).* **5)** *No, the comma is not accepted.* **6)** *No, putting a space before or after E is incorrect.* **7)** *Yes.* **8)** *No. Since the correct answer doesn't have a tolerance, the student's inexact answer is not accepted.* **9)** *Yes.*